Also by Henri Cole

Blizzard 2020

Orphic Paris 2018

Nothing to Declare 2015

Touch 2011

Pierce the Skin: Selected Poems, 1982–2007 2010

Blackbird and Wolf 2007

Middle Earth 2003

The Visible Man 1998

The Look of Things 1995

The Zoo Wheel of Knowledge 1989

The Marble Queen 1986

GRAVITY AND CENTER

GRAVITY AND CENTER

SELECTED SONNETS, 1994–2022

HENRI COLE

FARRAR STRAUS GIROUX — NEW YORK

CO

Farrar, Straus and Giroux
120 Broadway, New York 10271

Library of Congress Cataloging-in-Publication Data
Names: Cole, Henri, author.
Title: Gravity and center : selected sonnets, 1994–2022 / Henri Cole.
Description: First edition. | New York : Farrar Straus Giroux, 2023. | Includes index.
Identifiers: LCCN 2022055018 | ISBN 9780374606688 (hardcover)
Subjects: LCGFT: Sonnets. | Poetry.
Classification: LCC PS3553.04725 G73 2023 | DDC 811/.54—dc23/eng/20221114
LC record available at https://lccn.loc.gov/2022055018

Designed by Crisis

Our books may be purchased in bulk for promotional,
educational, or business use. Please contact your local
bookseller or the Macmillan Corporate and Premium
Sales Department at 1-800-221-7945, extension 5442,
or by email at MacmillanSpecialMarkets@macmillan.com.

www.fsgbooks.com
www.twitter.com/fsgbooks
www.facebook.com/fsgbooks

10 9 8 7 6 5 4 3 2 1

JUN 1 5 2023

FOR CLAIRE MALROUX

I came from a place with a hole in it,
my body once its body, behind a beard of hair.
And after I emerged, all dripping wet,
heavy drops came out of my eyes, touching its face.
I kissed its mouth; I bit it with my gums.
I lay on it like a snail on a cup,
my body, whatever its nature was,
revealed to me by its body. I did not know
I was powerless before a strange force.
I did not know life cheats us. All I knew,
nestling my head in its soft throat pouch,
was a hard, gemlike feeling burning through me,
like limbs of burning sycamores, touching
across some new barrier of touchability.

Contents

III. from *Blackbird and Wolf*

IV. from *Touch*

V. from *Blizzard*

VI. New Poems

I

FROM

THE

VISIBLE

MAN

Arte Povera

In the little garden of Villa Sciarra,
I found a decade of poetry dead.
In the limestone fountain lay lizards
and Fanta cans, where Truth once splashed from The Source.

How pleased I was and defiant because
a dry basin meant the end of description & rhyme,
which had nursed and embalmed me at once.
Language was more than a baroque wall-fountain.

Nearby, a gas-light shone its white-hot tongue,
a baby spat up—the stomach's truthtelling—
a mad boy made a scene worthy of Stalin.
Ah, to see the beast shitting in its cage!

Then the lying—"Yes sir, Daddy"—which changes nothing.
My soul-animal prefers the choke-chain.

White Spine

Liar, I thought, kneeling with the others,
how can He love me and hate what I am?
The dome of St. Peter's shone yellowish
gold, like butter and eggs. "My God," I prayed
anyhow, as if made in the image
and likeness of Him. Nearby, a handsome
priest looked at me like a stone; I looked back,
not desiring to go it alone.
The college of cardinals wore punitive red.
The white spine waved to me from his white throne.
Being in a place not my own, much less myself,
I climbed out, a beast in a crib.
Somewhere a terrorist rolled a cigarette.
Reason, not faith, would change him.

Adam Dying

(Piero della Francesca, *Death of Adam*,
Arezzo, Basilica of San Francesco)

Though the most we can say is that it is
as if there were a world before Adam,
even that seems narrow and parochial
as we contemplate his dying . . . while Eve,
with withered breasts, watches pensively,
and the mellifluous young, in animal skins,
stand about emotionless, like pottery.
What do the significant glances mean?

Can only Adam—naked, decrepit,
sprawled in the dirt—see what dying is?
How can they not hear the moaning, smell the body,
suffer the burden of original sin?
East & West, armies revile each other.
Mothers hunt among the decomposing dead.

from **Chiffon Morning**

I

I am lying in bed with my mother,
where my father seldom lay. Little poem,
help me to say all I need to say, better.
Hair dyed, combed; nails polished; necklacelike scar
ear-to-ear; stocky peasant's bulk hidden
under an unfeminine nightgown; sour-milk
breaths rehearsing death, she faces me, her room
a pill museum where orange tea bags
draining on napkins almost pass for art.
Even the Christmas amaryllis sags
under the weight of its blood-red
petals, unfolding like a handkerchief.
From the television screen, a beauty-
pageant queen waves serenely at me.

II

In the oily black barbecue smoke,
in our blue Chevrolet station wagon,
in a cottage at the sea, no one spoke
but me to the nerveless God
who never once stopped their loveless act:
the cursing mouths, the shoving and choking,
the violent pulse, the wrecked hair, the hunchbacked
reprisal, the suddenly inverted sky,
the fiendish gasping, the blade that cuts all
understanding, the white knuckles, the fly
remarkably poised on a blue throat.
I try to pity them. Perhaps God did
on those occasions when battle was a prelude
to sex, and peace, like an arrow, found us.

V

As the cuckoo clock crows in the kitchen,
on her nightstand others as bluntly chime
but cannot break her drugged oblivion.
Please wake up, Mother, and wet your cottonmouth.
"She was agitated," nurses whispered
when we found her tied to the bed, knocked out.
Demerol blocked the pain, entering through the eyes,
while the mind, crushed like a wineglass, healed.
"I'll bury you all," she gloated, at home again.
Months later, they stitched her throat in surgery.
The voice that had been on the radio
when the war was on plunged a tragic octave.
More pills crowded her daily glass of milk.
My guilt seemed vain compared to what she felt.

VI

Mother is naked and holding me up
above her as soap streams from my face
(I'm wearing a dumb ape's frown) into the tub
where she is seated: the mind replays
what nurtures it. The black months when she
would lie assassinated like our Siamese cat
are still far off. Yet, tranced by a lush light,
which no one else sees, like a leaden bee
shackled to a poppy, I am not free.
Each time I am dunked in the green, green
sacramental water, I glare shamelessly
as she shrieks and kisses me, gripped in air;
I do not know if she loves me or cares,
if it's suffering or joy behind her tears.

Peonies

Ample creamy heads beaten down vulgarly,
as if by some deeply sado-masochistic impulse,
like the desire to subdue, which is normal and active,
and the desire for suffering, which is not;
papery white featherings stapled to long stalks,
sopped with rain and thrown about violently,
as Paul was from his horse by the voice of Christ,
as those he judged & condemned were, leaving the Earth;
and, deeper in, tight little buds that seem to blush
from the pleasure they take in being submissive,
because absolute humility in the face of cruelty
is the Passive's way of becoming himself;
the groan of it all, like a penetrated body—
those of us who hear it know the feeling.

II

FROM

MIDDLE

EARTH

Icarus Breathing

Indestructible seabirds, black and white, leading and following;
semivisible mist, undulating, worming about the head;
rain starring the sea, tearing all over me;
our little boat, as in a Hokusai print, nudging closer
to Icarus (a humpback whale, not a foolish dead boy)
heaving against rough water; a voluminous inward grinding—
like a self breathing, but not a self—revivifying,
oxygenating the blood, making the blowhole move,
like a mouth silent against the decrees of fate: joy, grief,
desperation, triumph. Only God can obstruct them.
A big wave makes my feet slither. I feel like a baby,
bodiless and strange: a man is nothing if he is not changing.
Father, is that you breathing? Forgiveness is anathema to me.
I apologize. Knock me to the floor. Take me with you.

The Hare

The hare does not belong to the rodents;
he is a species apart. Holding him firmly
against my chest, kissing his long white ears,
tasting earth on his fur and breath,
I am plunged into that white sustenance again,
where a long, fathomless calm emerges—
like a love that is futureless but binding
for a body on a gurney submerged in bright light,
as an orchard is submerged in lava—
while the hand of my brother, my companion
in nothingness, strokes our father,
but no power in the air touches us,
as one touches those one loves, as I
stroke a hare trembling in a box of straw.

Kayaks

Beyond the soggy garden, two kayaks
float across mild clear water. A red sun
stains the lake like colored glass. Day is stopping.
Everything I am feels distant or blank
as the opulent rays pass through me,
distant as action is from thought,
or language is from all things desirable
in the world, when it does not deliver
what it promises and pathos comes instead—
the same pathos I feel when I tell myself,
within or without valid structures of love:
I have been deceived, he is not what he seemed—
though the failure is not in the other,
but in me because I am tired, hurt, or bitter.

Casablanca Lily

It has the odor of Mother leaving
when I was a boy. I watch the back
of her neck, wanting to cry, "Come back. Come back!"
So it is the smell of not saying what I feel,
of irrationality intruding
upon the orderly, of experience
seeking me out, though I do not want it to.

Unnaturally white with auburn anthers,
climbing the invisible ladder from birth
to death, it reveals the whole poignant
superstructure of itself without piety,
like Mother pushing a basket down
the grocery aisle, her pungent vital body
caught in the stranglehold of her mind.

Veil

We were in your kitchen eating sherbet
to calm the fever of a summer day.
A bee scribbled its essence between us,
like a minimalist. A boy hoed manure
in the distance. The surgical cold of ice
made my head ache, then a veil was lifted.
Midday sprayed the little room with gold,
and I thought, Now I am awake. Now
freedom is lifting me out of the abyss
of coming and going in life without thinking,
which is the absence of freedom. Now I see
the still, black eyes saying, *Someone wants you,
not me.* Now nothing is hidden. Now,
water and soil are striving to be flesh.

Swans

From above we must have looked like ordinary
tourists feeding winter swans, though it was
the grit of our father we flung hard
into the green water slapping against the pier,
where we stood soberly watching the ash float
or acquiesce and the swans, mooring themselves
against the little scrolls churned up out of the grave
by a motorboat throbbing in the distance.
What we had in common had been severed
from us. Like an umbrella in sand, I stood
rigidly apart—the wind flashing its needles
in air, the surf heavy, nebulous—remembering
a sunburned boy napping between hairy legs,
yellow jackets hovering over an empty basket.

Radiant Ivory

After the death of my father, I locked
myself in my room, bored and animal-like.
The travel clock, the Johnnie Walker bottle,
the parrot tulips—everything possessed his face,
chaste and obscure. Snow and rain battered the air
white, insane, slathery. Nothing poured
out of me except sensibility, dilated.
It was as if I were *sub*-born—preverbal,
truculent, pure—with hard ivory arms
reaching out into a dark and crowded space,
illuminated like a perforated silver box
or a little room in which glowing cigarettes
came and went, like souls losing magnitude,
but none with the battered hand I knew.

Black Camellia

(after Petrarch)

Little room, with four and a half tatami mats
and sliding paper doors, that used to be
a white, translucent place to live in refined poverty,
what are you now but scalding water in a bath?
Little mattress, that used to fold around me
at sunrise as unfinished dreams were fading,
what are you now but a blood-red palanquin
of plucked feathers and silk airing in the sun?
Weeding the garden, paring a turnip, drinking tea
for want of wine, I flee from my secret love
and from my mind's worm—This is a poem.
Is this a table? No, this is a poem. Am I a girl?—
seeking out the meat-hook crowd I once loathed,
I'm so afraid to find myself alone.

Landscape with Deer and Figure

If you listen, you can hear them chewing
before you see them standing or sitting—
with slim legs and branching antlers—
eating together like children, or the souls
of children, no one animal his own,
as I am my own, watching them watch me,
feeling a fever mount in my forehead,
where all that I am is borne and is effaced
by a herd of deer gathered in the meadow—
like brown ink splashed on rice paper—
abstract, exalted, revealing the eternal harmony,
for only five or six moments, of obligation to family
manifested with such frightful clarity and beauty
it quells the blur of human feeling.

Green Shade

(Nara Deer Park)

With my head on his spotted back
and his head on the grass—a little bored
with the quiet motion of life
and a cluster of mosquitoes making
hot black dunes in the air—we slept
with the smell of his fur engulfing us.
It was as if my dominant functions were gazing
and dreaming in a field of semiwild deer.
It was as if I could dream what I wanted,
and what I wanted was to long for nothing—
no facts, no reasons—never to say again,
"I want to be like him," and to lie instead
in the hollow deep grass—without esteem or riches—
gazing into the big, lacquer black eyes of a deer.

Kyushu Hydrangea

Some might say there are too many
for a charity hospital, too many pale
pink blossoms opening into creamy
paler ones, just when everything else
is dying in the garden. They can't see
the huge, upright panicles correspond
to something else, something not external at all,
but its complement, that atmosphere of pure
unambiguous light burning inwardly,
not in self-regard but in self-forgetting;
they can't see the lush rainy-season flowers,
with feet planted partially in rock,
lifting their big solemn heads over
the verdant wounded hands of the leaves.

Crows in Evening Glow

The terrible glorious crows are convening again,
swooping into the area with triumphant caws,
plunging with demon black wings from utility poles,
kicking and pecking a neighbor's kittens.
Wearing the plaid shirt that was my father's plaid shirt,
I throw a tarp over a pile of clear pink
hemorrhaging garbage bags. See a crow,
take three steps back. Three crows cried,
someone has died. "Go home, Crows!" I holler,
"My black-lipped daddy is gone." Poor crows,
perplexing as men, nobody is listening
to their tired signals, not even the mother,
with blue drooping breast, nursing a newborn
under a red maple with a nest.

Necessary and Impossible

It is a nation born in the quiet part of the mind,
that has no fantasy of omnipotence,
no God but nature, no net of one vow,
no dark corner of the poor, no fugue-work of hate,
no hierarchies of strength, knowledge, or love,
no impure water spasming from rock, no swarm of polluted flies,
no ash-heap of concrete, gypsum, and glass,
no false mercy or truths buried in excrement;
and in this nation of men and women,
no face in the mirror reflecting more darkness
than light, more strife than love, no more strife
than in my hands now, as I sit on a rock,
tearing up bread for red and white carp
pushing out of their element into mine.

Cleaning the Elephant

Thirsty and pale, her face lowered in concentration,
she doesn't seem to mind my sweeping
insects and dung from her corrugated flesh,
permitting me even to brush her soft hairy nape,
where I dream of squatting barefoot one day,
like a figure in a scroll, to feel the immutable
place of thought, if an elephant has thought.
"What is the smell of being human?" I want to ask,
like Plato, desiring to witness the truth
as both elephant and embodiment,
pushing out everything else—as when a soul,
finding its peculiar other, pushes out
the staple of life, which is suffering,
and a red sun wraps everything in gold.

Morning Glory

Out my window, in a garden the size of an urn,
a morning glory is climbing toward me.
It is 5 a.m. on the ninth day of the seventh month.
Lying on my soft mats, like a long white rabbit,
I can feel the purifying flames of summer
denuding the landscape, not of birds and animals,
but of blame and illusion. I can hear the white
splashing rivers of forgetfulness and oblivion
soaking me all at once, like loving a man
without wanting him, or a baby emerging
under white light out of its mother,
not the artificial light of the hospital corridor
but of joy growing wild in the garden, its pallid blue
trumpets piercing a brocade of red leaves.

Myself with Cats

Hanging out the wash, I visit the cats.
"I don't belong to nobody," Yang insists vulgarly.
"Yang," I reply, "you don't know nothing."
Yin, an orange tabby, agrees
but puts kindness ahead of rigid truth.
I admire her but wish she wouldn't idolize
the one who bullies her. I once did that.
Her silence speaks needles when Yang thrusts
his ugly tortoiseshell body against hers,
sprawled in my cosmos. "Really, I don't mind,"
she purrs—her eyes horizontal, her mouth
an Ionian smile, her legs crossed nobly
in front of her, a model of cat Nirvana—
"withholding his affection, he made me stronger."

Pillowcase with Praying Mantis

I found a praying mantis on my pillow.
"What are you praying for?" I asked. "Can you pray
for my father's soul, grasping after Mother?"
Swaying back and forth, mimicking the color
of my sheets, raising her head like a dragon's,
she seemed to view me with deep feeling, as if I were
St. Sebastian bound to a Corinthian column
instead of just Henri lying around reading.
I envied her crisp linearity, as she galloped
slow motion onto my chest, but then she started
mimicking me, lifting her arms in an attitude
of a scholar thinking or romantic suffering.
"Stop!" I sighed, and she did, flying in a wide arc,
like a tiny god-horse hunting for her throne room.

Melon and Insects

Pedaling home at twilight, I collided
with a red dragonfly, whose tiny boneless
body was thrown into my bicycle-basket.
In my bed, in a pocket notebook, I made
a drawing, then cried, "Wake up, Dragonfly.
Don't die!" I was sitting half-naked
in the humidity, my pen in my hot palm.
I was smiling at Dragonfly, but getting angry.
So I put him in a rice bowl, with some melon
and swept-up corpses of mosquitoes,
where he shone like a big broken earring,
his terrified eyes gleaming like little suns,
making me exhausted, lonely like that,
before sleep, waiting to show my drawing.

Insomnia

At night by lamplight certain insects,
floating or flying, in black or red or gold,
emerge like actors, vaguely apparitional,
in the ordinary space of my room.
Last night, they did *The Tempest* in a frenzy,
demanding I play Prospero and forgive
everyone. "What is this!" I moaned.
Dear unnatural Ariel, I loved him,
the island setting, the auspicious revenge—
how could I resist? The rain came down,
filling up time like sand or human understanding.
It was as if I were dreaming or dead.
I forgave my brother; he forgave me.
We huddled together in the dark backward of the night.

Original Face

Some mornings I wake up kicking like a frog.
My thighs ache from going nowhere all night.
I get up—tailless, smooth-skinned, eyes protruding—
and scrub around for my original face.
It is good I am dreaming, I say to myself.
The real characters and events would hurt me.
The real lying, shame, and envy would turn
even a pleasure-loving man into a stone.
Instead, my plain human flesh wakes up
and gazes out at real sparrows skimming the luminous
wet rooftops at the base of a mountain.
No splayed breasts, no glaring teeth, appear before me.
Only the ivory hands of morning touching
the real face in the real mirror on my bureau.

Mask

I tied a paper mask onto my face,
my lips almost inside its small red mouth.
Turning my head to the left, to the right,
I looked like someone I once knew, or was,
with straight white teeth and boyish bangs.
My ordinary life had come as far as it would,
like a silver arrow hitting cypress.
Know your place or you'll rue it, I sighed
to the mirror. To succeed, I'd done things
I hated; to be loved, I'd competed promiscuously:
my essence seemed to boil down to only this.
Then I saw my own hazel irises float up,
like eggs clinging to a water plant,
seamless and clear, in an empty, pondlike face.

My Tea Ceremony

Oh, you bowls, don't tell the others I drink
my liquor out of you. I want a feeling of beauty
to surround the plainest facts of my life.
Sitting on my bare heels, making a formal bow,
I want an atmosphere of gentleness to drive
out the squalor of everyday existence
in a little passive house surrounded
by black rocks and gray gravel.
Half-cerebral, half-sensual, I want to hear
the water murmuring in the kettle
and to see the spider, green as jade,
remaining aloof on the wall.

                                                 Heart, unquiet thing,
I don't want to hate anymore. I want love
to trample through my arms again.

Fish and Watergrass

My heart and my body were separate,
when I got off my bike, soaked with sweat,
and put my face in the river, an ethereal
dark place full of algae and watergrass.
Unable to keep a tight control over
their coal-black bodies in the current,
a cluster of koi groped forward,
with white, translucent, overworked eyes
searching for something, as a man searches
after going a great distance.
                              Who were you
that even now all of me is in tatters,
aching to touch your face floating in dream,
defining itself, like a large white
flower, by separation from me?

Olympia

Tired, hungry, hot, I climbed the steep slope
to town, a sultry, watery place, crawling with insects
and birds.
      In the semidarkness of the mountain,
small things loomed large: a donkey urinating on a palm;
a salt-and-saliva-stained boy riding on his mother's back;
a shy roaming black Adam. I was walking on an edge.
The moments fused into one crystalline rock,
like ice in a champagne bucket. Time was plunging forward,
like dolphins scissoring open water or like me,
following Jenny's flippers down to see the coral reef,
where the color of sand, sea, and sky merged,
and it was as if that was all God wanted:
not a wife, a house, or a position,
but a self, like a needle, pushing in a vein.

Blur

Little Lamb,
Here I am,
Come and lick
My white neck.
—William Blake, "Spring"

1.

It was a Christian idea, sacrificing
oneself to attain the object of one's desire.
I was weak and he was like opium to me,
so present and forceful. I believed I saw myself
through him, as if in a bucket being drawn
up a well, cold and brown as tea.
My horse was wet all that summer.
I pushed him, he pushed me back—proud, lonely,
disappointed—until I rode him,
or he rode me, in tight embrace, and life went on.
I lay whole nights—listless, sighing, gleaming
like a tendril on a tree—withdrawn
into some desiccated realm of beauty.
The hand desired, but the heart refrained.

2.

The strong sad ritual between us could not be broken:
the empathetic greeting; the apologies
and reproaches; the narrow bed of his flesh;
the fear of being shown whole in the mirror
of another's fragmentation; the climbing on;
the unambiguous freedom born of submission;
the head, like a rock, hefted on and off moist earth;
the rough language; the impermeable core
of one's being made permeable; the black hair
and shining eyes; and afterward, the marrowy
emissions, the gasping made liquid; the torso,
like pale clay or a plank, being dropped;
the small confessional remarks that inscribe
the soul; the indolence; the being alone.

3.

Then everything decanted and modulated,
as it did in a horse's eye, and the self—
pure, classical, like a figure carved from stone—
was something broken off again.
Two ways of being: one, seamless
saturated color (not a bead of sweat),
pure virtuosity, bolts of it; the other,
raw and unsocialized, "an opera of impurity,"
like super-real sunlight on a bruise.
I didn't want to have to choose.
It didn't matter anymore what was true
and what was not. Experience was not facts,
but uncertainty. Experience was not events,
but feelings, which I would overcome.

4.

Waking hungry for flesh, stalking flesh
no matter where—in the dunes, at the Pantheon,
in the Tuileries, at the White Party—
cursing and fumbling with flesh, smelling flesh,
clutching flesh, sucking violently on flesh,
cleaning up flesh, smiling at flesh, running away
from flesh, and later loathing flesh,
half of me was shattered, half was not,
like a mosaic shaken down by earthquake.
All the things I loved—a horse, a wristwatch,
a hall mirror—and all the things I endeavored to be—
truthful, empathetic, funny—presupposed
a sense of self locked up in a sphere,
which would never be known to anyone.

5.

Running, lifting, skipping rope at the gym,
I was a man like a bronze man;
I was my body—with white stones
in my eye sockets, soldered veins in my wrists,
and a delicately striated, crepelike scrotum.
Sighs, grunts, exhales, salt stains, dingy mats,
smeared mirrors, and a faintly sour smell
filled the gulf between the mind and the world,
but the myth of love for another remained
bright and plausible, like an athlete painted
on the slope of a vase tying his sandal.
In the showers, tears fell from our hair,
as if from bent glistening sycamores.
It was as if Earth were taking us back.

6.

In front of me, you are sleeping. I sleep also.
Probably you are right that I project
the ambiguities of my own desires.
I feel I only know you at the edges.
Sometimes in the night I jump up panting,
see my young gray head in the mirror,
and fall back, as humans do, from the cold glass.
I don't have the time to invest in what
I purport to desire. But when you open
your eyes shyly and push me on the shoulder,
all I am is impulse and longing
pulled forward by the rope of your arm,
I, flesh-to-flesh, sating myself
on blurred odors of the soft black earth.

III

FROM

BLACKBIRD

AND

WOLF

Gulls

Naked, hairy, trembling, I dove into the green,
where I saw a bulky form that was Mother
in her pink swimsuit, pushing out of water,
so I kicked deeper, beyond a sugar boat
and Blake's Ulro and Beulah; beyond grief, fate;
fingers, toes, and skin; beyond speech,
plagues of the blood, and flowers thrown on a coffin;
beyond Eros and the disease of incompleteness;
and as I swam I saw myself against the sky
and against the light, a tiny human knot with eyes,
my numb hands and repeated motion, like the gulls aloft,
touching the transparent structure of the world,
and in that icy, green, silvery frothing,
I was straightening all that I had made crooked.

Oil & Steel

My father lived in a dirty-dish mausoleum,
watching a portable black-and-white television,
reading the Encyclopaedia Britannica,
which he preferred to Modern Fiction.
One by one, his schnauzers died of liver disease,
except the one that guarded his corpse
found holding a tumbler of Bushmills.
"Dead is dead," he would say, an anti-preacher.
I took a plaid shirt from the bedroom closet
and some motor oil—my inheritance.
Once, I saw him weep in a courtroom—
neglected, needing nursing—this man who never showed
me much affection but gave me a knack
for solitude, which has been mostly useful.

Ambulance

Gentleness had come a great distance to be there,
I thought, as paramedics stanched the warm blood,
signaling one another with their eyes.
I was not as I was, and I didn't know why,
so I was aware of a shattering, of an unbidden,
moving under the influence of a restoring force.
Like a Japanese fan folding, my spirit seemed possessed
of such a simple existence, the sexual principle
no longer at its center, nor memory.
I felt like the personification of an abstraction,
like mercy. My hands were red and swollen.
A great chain, the twitch of my life, dragged against decay.
Then I heard shouts. Far off, a horse whinnied.
I blinked back tears as I was lifted forth.

Maple Leaves Forever

I didn't know what to do with myself,
arriving through woods and fields at the lake.
The world of instinct, crying out at night
(its grief so human), frightened me,
so I scribbled vainly, contemplating the surface
of the water, frolicking in it until my long,
amphibious body, covered in fine hairs—
with whiskers, moles, and a blunt nose—
became terra cotta brown, and I—usually nocturnal—
slept all night and ate omnivorously
(eggs, fish, berries, and honey), and, after a few weeks,
the puny ingredients of my life vanished.
I, upright on hind legs, alternatively sexed
(even that seemed banal), didn't want to go home.

Migraine

As I light the oven to warm up dinner,
I watch a fly make an exploration
of the room, where I've hung wet clothes.
My human fingers, with their long, slender bones,
appear more like a reptile's. I don't know,
perhaps there's no meaning in all this,
like a slit in the grassy earth, from which rodents
come and go. Mud and life, water and hope—
I want them all, really. Instead, I listen
to a blood-dyed fist *tap-tap* inside my skull
and entertain a miserable fly.
In a short while, he'll run down,
like my wristwatch, but my warm human breath
will make him fly again.

To Sleep

Then out of the darkness leapt a bare hand
that stroked my brow, "Come along, child;
stretch out your feet under the blanket.
Darkness will give you back, unremembering.
Do not be afraid." So I put down my book
and pushed like a finger through sheer silk,
the autobiographical part of me, the *am*,
snatched up to a different place, where I was
no longer my body but something more—
the compulsive, disorderly parts of me
in a state of equalization, everything sliding off:
war, suicide, love, poverty—as the rebellious,
mortal I, I, I lay, like a beetle irrigating a rose,
my red thoughts in a red shade all I was.

The Tree Cutters

You can't see them and then you can,
like bear cubs in the treetops working for man,
hoisting one another with ropes and pulleys
that seem the clearest possible metaphor
for bright feelings vs. dark feelings,
as I lie in the grass below, hearing the big limbs fall,
like lightning exploding on the lake.

Once, a thick, dirty, bad-smelling sorrow
covered me like old meat: I saw a blood-stained toad,
instead of my white kitten; I saw shadows and misprision,
instead of my milk and pancakes. "Maybe God has gone away,"
my life moaned, hugging my knees, my teeth, my terrible pride,
though, after a time, like a warm chrysalis, it produced
a tough, lustrous thread the pale yellow of onions.

Birthday

When I was a boy, we called it punishment
to be locked up in a room. God's apparent
abdication from the affairs of the world
seemed unforgivable. This morning,
climbing five stories to my apartment,
I remember my father's angry voice
mixed with anxiety and love. As always,
the possibility of home—at best an ideal—
remains illusory, so I read Plato, for whom love
has not been punctured. I sprawl on the carpet,
like a worm composting, understanding things
about which I have no empirical knowledge.
Though the door is locked, I am free.
Like an outdated map, my borders are changing.

Gravity and Center

I'm sorry I cannot say I love you when you say
you love me. The words, like moist fingers,
appear before me full of promise but then run away
to a narrow black room that is always dark,
where they are silent, elegant, like antique gold,
devouring the thing I feel. I want the force
of attraction to crush the force of repulsion
and my inner and outer worlds to pierce
one another, like a horse whipped by a man.
I don't want words to sever me from reality.
I don't want to need them. I want nothing
to reveal feeling but feeling—as in freedom,
or the knowledge of peace in a realm beyond,
or the sound of water poured in a bowl.

American Kestrel

I see you sitting erect on my fire escape,
plucking at your dinner of flayed mouse,
like the red strings of a harp, choking a bit
on the venous blue flesh and hemorrhaging tail.
With your perfect black-and-white thief's mask,
you look like a stuffed bird in a glass case,
somewhere between the animal and human life.
The love word is far away. Can you see me?
I am a man. No one has what I have:
my long clean hands, my bored lips. This is my home:
Woof-woof, the dog utters, afraid of emptiness,
as I am, so my soul attaches itself to things,
trying to create something neither confessional
nor abstract, like the moon breaking through the pines.

Quarry

This is the time of year the missing ones
come back to us—no longer weighted down
by debris, curled into fetal positions,
rising naked through the murky water—
as if they can hear our yelling shouts
as we dive from the ledges above,
pretending they are not there.
Life piles onto life. "Come," says
the onyx water, "come into my deep,"
and I run across the grass into the fizzy air—
insane, undignified—but even there,
falling through the lavender haze, I extend
my arms to you, my secret comrade,
who made me love you.

Homosexuality

First I saw the round bill, like a bud;
then the sooty-crested head, with avernal eyes
flickering, distressed, then the peculiar
long neck wrapping and unwrapping itself,
like pity or love, when I removed the stovepipe
cover of the bedroom chimney to free
what was there and a duck crashed into the room
(I am here in this fallen state), hitting her face,
bending her throat back (my love, my inborn
turbid wanting, at large all night), backing away,
gnawing at her own wing linings (the poison of my life,
the beast, the wolf), leaping out the window,
which I held open (now clear, sane, serene),
before climbing back naked into bed with you.

Haircut

I sit on the dock for a haircut and watch
as summer spreads out, relieving the general,
indiscriminate gray, like a mouthful of gin
spreading out through the capillaries
of my brain, etherizing everything
it is too painful to think or say,
as I dangle my feet in the water,
like bits of a man. On the goldenrod,
Japanese beetles are holding an orgy.
The green snake throws off its enameled skin.
And somewhere—invisible as the avenues
of the dead—a small door is left open for love,
pushing and pulling at each of us, as the water
pushes and pulls at my cut gray hairs.

Toxicology

Here, all night, in locked Ward C, they arrive,
like moist, limp hands tied fast to nothing.
Asleep or awake, in the somber light
of dream or nocturnal data-processing,
life undeaths itself, as if it really were
a limitless map of transparent blue lines
leading us out of captivity,
out of the masochistic desire
to crush and be crushed in turn,
and out of paranoid dissembling.
Here, in the nightmare border country of overdoses—
where the worm's mouth sucks
and God, our Father, feeds the altar flame
—my task is to give, empathize, and love him.

Poppies

Waking from comalike sleep, I saw the poppies,
with their limp necks and unregimented beauty.
Pause, I thought, say something true: It was night,
I wanted to kiss your lips, which remained supple,
but all the water in them had been replaced
with embalming compound. So I was angry.
I loved the poppies, with their wide-open faces,
how they carried themselves, beckoning to me
instead of pushing away. The way in and the way out
are the same, essentially: emotions disrupting thought,
proximity to God, the pain of separation.
I loved the poppies, with their effortless existence,
like grief and fate, but tempered and formalized.
Your hair was black and curly; I combed it.

Bowl of Lilacs

My lilacs died today, floating in a bowl.
All week I watched them pushing away,
their pruned heads swollen together into something
like anger, making a brief comeback
toward the end, as if secretly embalmed.
Just before your death, I cut your hair,
so when you were laid out you looked like yourself.
Then some men screwed planks over your coffin.
I held a towel to my face. Once, in a light-bathed kitchen,
naked and blissfully myself, I scrambled us eggs
and felt the act of looking and perceiving
was no longer something understood
from the exterior. It was pure being:
saturated and raw as a bowl of lilacs.

Shaving

Outstretched in the tub, like a man in a tomb,
I pull the razor across my face and throat.
The bathroom is pristine, spare, without any clear
conflict; I like that. The cells in my skin
draw heat to themselves, like grape bunches.
In the silver hand mirror, my youthful
shyness is gone now. I lie bent, turned in,
but supple, pliant. I was rough on you;
I know this because you told me, but you
held up well. Trees, mammals, fire, snow—
they are like emotions. Through our eyes,
pain comes in (my doctor told me this),
but how does it exit, if you're looking forward
and I'm looking back, my big, unlovely head
(you called it that) feverish, then shivery?

My Weed

On the path to the water, I found an ugly weed
growing between rocks. The wind was stroking it,
saying, "My weed, my weed." Its solid,
hairy body rose up, with big silver leaves
that rubbed off on me, like sex. At first,
I thought it was a lamb's ear, but it wasn't.
I'm not a member of the ugly school,
but I circled around it and looked a lot,
which is to say, I was just being, and it seemed to me—
in a higher sense—to represent the sanity of living.
It was twilight. Planets were gathering.
"Mr. Weed," I said, "I'm competitive,
I'm afraid, I'm isolated, I'm bright.
Can you tell me how to survive?"

Self-Portrait with Red Eyes

Throughout our affair of eleven years,
disappearing into the pleasure-unto-death
acts I recall now as love and, afterward,
orbiting through the long, deep sleeps
in which memory, motor of everything,
reconstituted itself, I cared nothing about
life outside the walls of our bedroom.

The hand erasing writes the real thing,
and I am trying. I loved life and see now
this was a weakness. I loved the little
births and deaths occurring in us daily.
Even the white spit on your sharp teeth
was the foam of love, saying to me: *It is not true,
after all, that you were never loved.*

Embers

Poor summer, it doesn't know it's dying.
A few days are all it has. Still, the lake
is with me, its strokes of blue-violet
and the fiery sun replacing loneliness.
I feel like an animal that has found a place.
This is my burrow, my nest, my attempt
to say, "I exist." A rose can't shut itself
and be a bud again. It's a malady,
wanting it. On the shore, the moon sprinkles
light over everything, like a campfire,
and in the green-black night, the tall pines
hold their arms out as God held His arms
out to say that He was lonely and that
He was making Himself a man.

Wet Apples

As I lie on my belly at the edge of the dock,
I hear sighing, plainly human, from behind a membrane.
Daylight leaks yellow and black, then everything goes raw.
I'm a boy again, setting the jib but messing it up;
the sigh—thin, acidic, austere—is my father's;
then I hear others: the sighs of wet trees bending
with apples, of gnats on the lake, and of young furrows
at the corners of my eyes; the sighs of duckweed
and pampas grass, of my sweat-moistened shirt
drawing bees like a flower, and of the nine Hells
under me biting the spirit because reason is triumphing
over the senses—all blame forgotten—as I sprawl
on warm wooden boards in the shadow of autumn leaves,
watching you crawl through clear water toward me.

Beach Walk

I found a baby shark on the beach.
Seagulls had eaten his eyes. His throat was bleeding.
Lying on shell and sand, he looked smaller than he was.
The ocean had scraped his insides clean.
When I poked his stomach, darkness rose up in him,
like black water. Later, I saw a boy,
aroused and elated, beckoning from a dune.
Like me, he was alone. Something tumbled between us—
not quite emotion. I could see the pink
interior flesh of his eyes. "I got lost. Where am I?"
he asked, like a debt owed to death.
I was pressing my face to its spear-hafts.
We fall, we fell, we are falling. Nothing mitigates it.
The dark embryo bares its teeth and we move on.

Eating the Peach

Eating the peach, I feel like a murderer.
Time and darkness mean nothing to me,
moving forward and back with my white enameled teeth
and bloated tongue sating themselves on moist,
pulpy flesh. When I suck at the pit that resembles
a small mammal's skull, it erases all memory
of trouble and strife, of loneliness and the blindings
of erotic love, and of the blueprint of a world
in which man, hater of reason, cannot make
things right again. Eating the peach, I feel the long
wandering, my human hand—once fin and paw—
reaching through and across the allegory of Eden,
mud, boredom, and disease, to bees, solitude,
and a thousand hairs of grass blowing by chill waters.

Dead Wren

When I open your little gothic wings
on my whitewashed chest of drawers,
I almost fear you, as if today were my funeral.
Moment by moment, enzymes digest
your life into a kind of coffin liqueur.
Two flies, like coroners, investigate your feathers.
My clock is your obelisk, though only this morning
you lunged into my room, extravagant as Nero,
then, not seeing yourself in the sunlit glass,
struck it. Night—what beams does it clear away?
The rain falls. The sky is pained. All that breathes suffers.
Yet the waters of affliction are purifying.
The wounded soldier heals. There is new wine and oil.
Here, take my handkerchief as your hearse.

Hymn

After a stormy night, with thunder peals,
I went out for coffee and found a woman
in a wheelbarrow, speaking in a low voice
to no one in particular, the *is* of her life
wholly stripped away, her once pretty face
hardened into a triangle, and I thought:
What one wants, to be a person who fully loves,
seems so focused and pure. The sun hadn't risen.

Living things flew around. The city crept up,
like a green blade out of a chasm emitting
plumes of vapor. All the people of the world
seemed to look away as water drops fell on us
from air conditioners and a terrible instrument
struck down out of a depthless blue sky.

The Lost Bee

(Firing weapons in a prolonged fusillade,
attacking militants left fifty-eight dead.)

In the hills, a boy drove a donkey cart;
women carried bundles of sticks on their heads;
a dog's bark echoed off the ivory rock;
a lost bee, blood-sticky little almsman,
bathed in a water trough. If every man has a soul,
these had fled or were fermenting.
Free at least from all pain,
the stunted figures lay like rag dolls.
Broken eyeglasses, a tangled earring,
tawny footprints leading nowhere deep,
deep inside the birth colonnade:
The lowing heifer tugged to the altar 2,000
years ago now wore a sad human face.
Why must God always side with the brave?

Bees

Poured through the bees, the sunlight, like flesh
and spirit, emits a brightness pushing everything
else away except the bees' vibrating bronze bodies
riding the air as if on strings that flex
and kick back as they circle the hive outside
my window, where they are cheerful and careful
in their work, their audible bee-voices
in solidarity with summer, as it is getting on,
and all the leaves of the forest quiver toward
nothingness on Earth, where we are all fallen
and where we sin and betray in order
to love and where the germinating seeds
of the soul are watered by tears of loneliness,
fear, and emotional revenge.

Mirror

After a season of war, darkness retreated
into darkness, and I thought: Now things will be different.
Hunting for mushrooms at the lake, I found youthful
men and women sunning themselves, while rabbits
hopped about. Darkness had made everything brighter.
At home, I sautéed porcini in butter, with garlic and parsley.
The chaos of life synthesized into something beautiful.
Seepages of violence receded. Even the blackbirds,
squealing in long-haired willows, fused in my mind with love,
instead of giving sorrow sound. Then in the mirror,
my body shone silvery white, like an ember
(what was my life?), but it was only the naked,
simpler me remembering the old pain of seeing.
Like a juicy worm in straw, it wanted to be fed.

City Horse

At the end of the road from concept to corpse,

sucked out to sea and washed up again—

with uprooted trees, crumpled cars, and collapsed houses—

facedown in dirt, and tied to a telephone pole,

as if trying to raise herself still, though one leg is broken,

to look around at the grotesque unbelievable landscape,

the color around her eyes, nose, and mane (the dapples of roan,

a mix of white and red hairs) now powdery gray—

O wondrous horse; O delicate horse—dead, dead—

with a bridle still buckled around her cheeks—"She was more
    smarter than me,

she just wait," a boy sobs, clutching a hand to his mouth

and stroking the majestic rowing legs,

stiff now, that could not outrun

the heavy, black, frothing water.

IV

FROM

TOUCH

Solitude: The Tower

Long ago, I lived at the foot of the mountains,
where my parents lived when they were young.
Nearby, there was a daffodil farm, which I bicycled past
each day on my way to the supermarket.
Occasionally, there were earthquakes, but no one noticed.
At my desk, words and phrases grew only slowly,
like the embedded or basal portion of a hair,
tooth, nail, or nerve. As I looked at the empty page—
seeing into love, seeing into suffering,
seeing into madness—my head ached so,
dear reader, emotions toppling me in one
direction, then another, but writing this now,
sometimes in a rush, sometimes after drifting thought,
I feel happiness, I feel I am not alone.

Shrike

How brightly you whistle, pushing the long, soft
feathers on your rump down across the branch,
like the apron of a butcher, as you impale a cricket
on a meat hook deep inside my rhododendron.
Poor cricket can hardly stand the whistling,
not to speak of the brownish-red pecking
(couldn't you go a little easy?), but holds up
pretty good in a state of oneiric pain.
Once, long ago, when they were quarrelling about money,
Father put Mother's head in the oven.
Who are you? it pleaded from the hell mouth.
Upstairs in the bathroom, I drank water right out of the tap,
my lips on the faucet. Everything was shaking and bumping.
Earth was drawing me into existence.

Sunflower

When Mother and I first had the do-not-
resuscitate conversation, she lifted her head,
like a drooped sunflower, and said,
"Those dying always want to stay."
Months later, on the kitchen table,
Mars red gladiolus sang "Ode to Joy,"
and we listened. House flies swooped and veered
around us, like the Holy Spirit. "Nature
is always expressing something human,"
Mother commented, her mouth twisting,
as I plucked whiskers from around it.
"Yes, no, please." Tenderness was not yet dust.
Mother sat up, rubbed her eyes drowsily, her breaths
like breakers, the living man the beach.

Mechanical Soft

Walking yesterday in the cold, bright air,
I encountered fifteen horses marching
in a phalanx down the avenue. Long before
they were visible, I heard their shoes striking
the pavement, as language is sometimes audible
before sense arrives. I loved how the wind played
with their long, brushed tails. Though in a faraway
place, I was not a stranger. Mother is dying,
you see, and proximity to this death makes me
nostalgic for the French language. I am not
a typical son, I suppose, valuing happiness,
even while spooning mechanically soft pears—
like light vanishing—into the body whose tissue
once dissolved to create breast milk for me.

Mosquito Mother

You gave me a nice bite; I hope I didn't rip your wing off,
pushing you away. We were sitting by the window;
outside, there was rain on steroids. Your voice was so funny—
up, down; soft, loud—but distant, I thought, reading
my magazine. Then I felt your subtle knife touching me,
as if I were just some part of the scenery, and we sat
like that a long time, your moist red crown all shiny,
as if from effusions: milk, blood, tears, urine, semen.
Tell me, was I happier there in my loneliness,
you feeding on my arm (*Let go of the spirit departed*),
emotion dripping liquid morphine through me (*Nobody there*),
as when—poem, rope, torture—I couldn't look at the corpse
in the coffin with eyes closed (*Continue your life*)?
It was a subtle knife, too, cutting lipid yellow, until I pushed it away.

Dead Mother

All of life was there—love, death, memory—
as the eyes rolled back into the wrinkled sleeve
of the head, and five or six tears—profound,
unflinching, humane—ran out of her skull,
breathtakingly heroic, and tenderness (massaging
the arms, sponging the lips) morphed into a dog
howling under the bed, the bruised body that
had carried us, splaying itself now, not abstract,
but symbolic, like the hot-water bottle,
the plastic rosaries, the shoes in the wheelchair
("I'm ready to stretch out"), as dents and punctures
of the flesh—those gruesome flowers—a macabre tumor,
and surreal pain, changed into hallowed marble,
a lens was cleared, a coffer penetrated.

Broom

A starkly lighted room with a tangy iron odor;
a subterranean dankness; a metal showerhead hanging from the
     ceiling;
a scalpel, a trocar, a pump; a white marble table; a naked, wrinkled
body faceup on a sheet, with scrubbed skin, clean nails,
and shampooed hair; its mouth sewn shut, with posed lips,
its limbs massaged, its arteries drained, its stomach and intestines
     emptied;
a pale blue sweater, artificial pearls, lipstick, and rouge;
hands that once opened, closed, rolled, unrolled, rerolled, folded,
     unfolded,
turned, and returned, as if breathing silver, unselfing themselves
     now
(very painful); hands that once tore open, rended, ripped,
served, sewed, and stroked (very loving), pushing and butting now
with all their strength as their physiognomy fills with firming fluid;
hands once raucous, sublime, quotidian—now strange, cruel, neat;
hands that once chased me gruesomely with a broom, then brushed
     my hair.

Hens

It's good for the ego, when I call and they come
running, squawking, and clucking, because it's feed time,
and once again I can't resist picking up little Lazarus,
an orange-and-white pullet I adore. "Yes, yes, everything will be
okay," I say to her glaring mongrel face. Come September,
she'll begin to lay the blue-green eggs I love poached.
God dooms the snake to taste nothing but the dust
and the hen to 4,000 or so ovulations. Poor Lazarus,
last spring an intruder murdered her sisters and left her
garroted in the coop. There's a way the wounded
light up a dark rectangular space. Suffering becomes
the universal theme. Too soft, and you'll be squeezed;
too hard, and you'll be broken. Even a hen knows this,
posing on a manure pile, her body a stab of gold.

Taxidermied Fawn

When a soft projectile hits a fixed obstacle,
soft comes out of it badly. Over there,
in the bedroom, that's a fawn.
Salt, blood, and saliva are gone now.
Sleep and death have transported the lithe body,
folded legs, and tiny bumps on the head.
A minor smear on the white spots is the only
evidence of a violent passage from bridal innocence
to the whiteness of death, which is the absence
of everything, and, in the end, all there really is.
It's dark now, pitch dark. When you walk
through a beam of light, bending your head back,
I'm not scared. I think, Well, what a pretty body,
and then I remember you are dead.

Ulro

It's a myth, the push-pull thing, the polarity stuff,
the of-two-minds/left-brain-right-brain discussions.
The world is nothing but the scraping of a donkey,
so he took three Percocet and put a gun to his head.
Last night, I dreamed so strongly about it—
the people touching his arms and legs to see
if they should be calling an ambulance,
the unfamiliar faces right in front of his nose.
Who does not believe his lice are hoofed animals?
Who does not win renown by committing an atrocity?
Cigarettes, love, work, liquor, brooding, despair—
one thing not controlled can destroy a life. Jesus,
I miss him. Why did his eyes have no veils?
Why was the salt of wisdom no good to him?

Pig

Poor patient pig—trying to keep his balance,
that's all, upright on a flatbed ahead of me,
somewhere between Pennsylvania and Ohio,
enjoying the wind, maybe, against the tufts of hair
on the tops of his ears, like a Stoic at the foot
of the gallows, or, with my eyes heavy and glazed
from caffeine and driving, like a soul disembarking,
its flesh probably bacon now tipping into split
pea soup, or, more painful to me, like a man
in his middle years struggling to remain
vital and honest while we're all just floating
around accidental-like on a breeze.
What funny thoughts slide into the head,
alone on the interstate with no place to be.

Hairy Spider

There's nothing like a big, long-legged spider to embody
the mind's life-giving power, especially when her babies
run up and stroke her face (if she has a face). Soon it will storm
and all of them will drown. Still, I love to watch their web
    changing,
like this year's words for this year's language, not didactic,
but affective, while absorbing the secret vibrations from the world,
and I love it when she climbs across clear water and drags
some horsefly back, like Beelzebub, to her silk coffer.
There's something unsettling happening, I know, but it tests
the connections between everything. Can she see if I am climbing,
I wonder, or kneeling down here on the dock, day after day,
when it's time for reading and writing again, and a hairy spider—
ingenious, bashful, insolent, laborious, patient—observes
a man no different than a lily, a worm, a clod of clay?

Last Words

She wore blue slacks with a white blouse
and ate a meal of asparagus with strawberries.
When an officer asked if she had anything
to say, she replied, "No, sir," then closed her eyes,
as they strapped her shaved head to the chair.
A handful of protesters waited at the road,
where a witness reported what had gone off without
a hitch (except for a little white smoke that came
out of her right ankle where an electrode was
fastened) as 2,300 watts of electricity shot
through her. "The dead are content," he asserted.
Then a white hearse appeared at the prison gates,
carrying the body of the laughing, girlish nail salon
operator who'd put a pickax in her husband.

Legend

On a rise overlooking a valley

                    circled by blue metrical mountains,
where the river source lies,

          a collection of shabby dwellings around a church
became a town on a hill

        with a single gate, a few high windows, a deep moat,
and thick perimeter walls

      in which twenty or thirty families lived, self-sufficient,
the women spinning wool,

               the men hunting with nets and falconry,
until, without provocation,

                 their Lord was murdered in his sleep.
It takes a special charisma for one man to say to another,

                  "Go forth, kill and be killed."
Soon there were only a gaunt, arched pig

                grubbing among the stones,
a few cocks, and a weary hen.

          When an earthquake made the towers sway,
a young heir rebuilt them.

         Away with the battlements, away with the drawbridges.
Ditches and moats filled in and planted.

Windows and terraces opened.

The chapel renovated.

Flocks of sheep contributed wool and soft cheeses.

Oxen harrowed the fields.

Lives of the inhabitants prospered for a time,

while on another perch, a battlement rose,

and a warlord with a little white goat watched.

The Flagellation

(Piero della Francesca, *The Flagellation*,
Urbino, Galleria Nazionale delle Marche)

Soon they'll knock nails into him, but first there's this,
a lesson in perspective with two worlds coming together:
one gloomy and transgressive, let's call it super-real,
a world behind this world, in which a man is tied to
a column—his hair and beard unkempt, his body raw,
though not bleeding—muttering, "I am afraid to fall down,
but I will not be dominated"; the other world is surreally
calm, with saturated colors and costumes of the day,
a youth's head framed by a laurel tree, nothing
appearing larger than it is, so the eyes drift back
to the deviant, the melancholic, the real, emotion
punching through the rational—like Mother cat with five
kittens in her tummy purring in my lap now—
as a man for his beliefs receives blow after blow.

Quai aux Fleurs

I want to just keep on smearing butter
& jam on toast with a blunt knife
and licking foam from my espresso cup,
while listening to Lizzy and Tricia practice French,
but I'm a realist. Even the songbirds have levels
of mercury in their blood and feathers. Somewhere,
in the brightness against a wall, a soldier crouches—
sand in his hair, juices dripping from his body.
Here there is joy, like a hole with greenness coming
out of it, but there night pushes against the cylinder
of his gun. He probably has a knife, too, in the presence
of the incomprehensible, thrusting his belly
to the ground, feeling the strangeness throb in his blood
as he touches the scope to his cheek.

Orange Hole

The horses were so beautiful but the people
ugly. Why is that? Both seemed perfectly alive.
Both seemed to want to do what was asked of them
as bullets snapped hitting branches and rocks,
and a blast wave blew everything down.
I crouched against a boulder looking for safety,
returning fire, everything in dreamy slow motion,
orange smoke drifting out of the misty hole,
introducing the idea of beauty as a salve
and of aesthetics making something difficult accessible.
Alone in that box of crisscrossing lead—
my ears ringing, my skin pouring sweat—
I missed you. But it was a rather pleasant feeling
being waited for. I thought, God must be happy.

Sleeping Soldiers

(from a newspaper photograph)

Grow old. Buy a house. Have a baby. Love someone.
Sometimes there are substitutions. A historical torque
pulls us away. A dearest beloved—in a harbor, trench, or house—
lies begging for morphine (just fucking do it,
the best place is in the neck!). Run away? Fight the power?
"Oh, she was a good girl." "His daddy was enlisted.
The apple don't fall far from the tree."
                                    After operations South,
the soldiers are sleeping now, in various postures of weariness,
on an oriental carpet—knees tucked into their chests,
arms touching one another—everything all interwoven,
like something abstract deep within us—
a soul, maybe—bare-knuckled, but delicate, too,
like a scissored-out black cameo held up
to the light before it is cut deeper.

Bats

Each night they come back, chasing one another
among the fronds after gorging on papayas,
to drink from the swimming pool. With my sleep-
stiffened bones, I like to watch them, careening
into the bright pool lights, spattering the walls with pulp
and guano, like graffiti artists. Sometimes, when they meet,
they hit one another's furred wings—*Love thy neighbor*
like thyself—and then soar off again to drink
more bleached water. Sometimes, it seems as if
they are watching me, like a Styrofoam head
with a wig on it. "The patient reports that he has
been lonely all his life," one screams to the other.
I can hardly stand it and put my face in my hands,
as they dive to-and-fro through all their happiness.

Seaweed

I love the green and brown seaweed
floating freely on the surface of the water,
like a Jackson Pollock, or an enormous bed
in which the world is no longer a place
of rigid structures. I feel drawn to it but also
to the sea with all its gigantic beauty pushing
against us and below. I want to look at you
but I do not. The edge of the beach brims
with light that glides down around our legs
and then down into the folded depths,
from which the waves erupt, toppling us suddenly
into their undulating plash, connecting—
over a vast terrain of ditches—the salt of sweat,
the salt of tears, and the salt of the sea.

Passion

Climbing around the immense bronze lap
of Buddha, wearing only briefs, short white robes,
and zori, the priests appear on the verge of song,
mopping and washing his big hypnotized eyes,
the thick, caressable curls of his hair,
and the outstretched hand urging, "Here I am,
I am a hand," strengthening a feeling of being
in myself, as I wander around below,
inhaling the odor of it, and the summer sky
divides and glows, releasing big sparks of rain
that seem almost to bruise me, as I swallow
the hot mouthfuls, thinking, Our love has ended.
We only have a little time, darling. Let's read,
swim, and sleep in one another's arms.

One Animal

Do not show how jealous you are. Do not
show how much you care. Do not think the bunch
of flowers in his hand connects the hand to you.
Do not close your eyes and kiss the funny
lips. Do not twist your torso, touching yourself
like a monkey. Do not put your mouth
on the filthy place that changes everything.
Do not utter the monosyllable twice that is
the signature of dogdom. Do not, afterward,
appear mangy with old breath, scrutinizing
every hole. And do not think—touching his hair,
licking, sucking, and being sucked in the same
instant, no longer lonely—that you
are two animals perfect as one.

Laughing Monster

"Some people take and some people get took,"
my father used to say, and I just ignored him.
After all, he'd wake up and take a swig with his juice.
Years later, I watch you emerge from the bathroom,
having breathed your fix, and wonder what it feels like—
the mild euphoria, the expression of power on your face,
the burst of relaxation—a little mirror to mull over
the question "Who am I and why?" Lunging forward
to assume the positions so imprecise to our natures,
hunting the elusive laughing monster of contentment—
my lips numb from yours (it numbs u if it's real,
it numbs ur throat and nose, and it numbs u inside
if u put it in there)—slovenly, degraded, vain,
I wonder if I am the taker or being took?

Self-Portrait with Addict

You won't come to bed because you're
doing amphetamines again. There's no animal
that sleep-deprives itself like the human.
"Please," I say, repeating the monosyllable.
Rian-rian, the Chinese dog mutters. *Wan-wan*,
the French. Delta waves (they look like
mountains) indicate the start of deep sleep.
Or is it just the down stroking of love?
There is no place in the world—, oh, never mind.
This morning, my thoughts are disorderly,
like black hairs. Listening to you sleep,
I love the refractive gaze of the eyes.
Tell me, my love, marching forward,
how will I bear the mighty freedom?

Quilt

Little muslin sacks from chewing tobacco,
home-dyed in pink and yellow, pieced as a zigzag—
a lively recycling of materials seen often in the South—
with sturdy stitches and a two-color scheme,
like a temperature chart pulled up around me.
What temperature is Henri, the black sheep,
arriving unexpectedly with a new lover—alcoholic
and impetuous—jolting the rest of the family
into spasms of pity, resentment, and half-admiring
amazement at his sheer nerve? I'm sorry I broke
the Ming Dynasty jar and set Poppop's beard on fire.
I could actually be normal if the imagination
(unstable, disquieting, fragile) is the Father penetrating
the Mother and this is my Child-poem.

Doll

Thrown on the carpet with your legs awry—
broken, scalped, microwaved—a receptacle
of love, you make me think the soul is larger
than the body. He lay like that the last time
I saw him, inhaling powder through a straw.
Studies show monkeys prefer it to the food
in their cages; this happens even when the monkeys
are starving. "You are all darkness," he used to say,
"and I am light." Though I understood this alertness
as compassion, it wasn't.

                        It's March now;
the light is brittle, hard, frozen.
Experience seems to come from a distance.
Waiting for spring thaw, I throw you
in a box with the others.

Resistance

Why didn't I tell you before? I'm telling
you now. I didn't go to him for virtue.
I liked the sound of someone else breathing.
I wanted to know what it felt like, eating honey
like a wasp. "Loser old man u r a cheap cunt,"
he wrote, "I need coke. Unless ur buying,
answer is no." Now, the whole insane,
undignified attempt at loving him is over,
the horrible sticky body that was mine
is mahogany in daylight. I intended to make
a poem about the superiority of language over
brute force, but this came instead: "Sleep sleep sleep,
no more wasting my ass with ur sleep." Still, entering
the room, I felt liquid, my eyes cleared.

Away

If I close my eyes, I see you again in front of me,
like light attracting light to itself. I'm standing
in the lake, forming a whirlpool with my arms,
letting the force of atonement pull me into its center
until I cannot any longer hang on to my observations
or any sense of myself, like dust and hydrogen clouds
getting all excited while creating new stars to light
the backyard. How poignantly emptiness cries out
to be filled.

        But writing this now, my hand is warm.
The character I call Myself isn't lustful, heavy,
melancholic. It's as if emotions are no longer bodied.
Eros isn't ripping through darkness. It's as if I'm
a boy again, observing the births of two baby lambs.
The world has just come into existence.

Carwash

I love the iridescent tricolor slime
that squirts all over my Honda in random
yet purposeful patterns as I sit in the semi-
dark of the "touch-free" carwash with you.
Listening to the undercarriage blast, I think,
Love changes and will not be commanded.
I smile at the long, flesh-colored tentacles waving
at us like passengers waving good-bye.
Water isn't shaped like a river or ocean;
it mists invisibly against metal and glass.
In the corridor of green unnatural lights
recalling the lunatic asylum, how can I
defend myself against what I want?
Lay your head in my lap. Touch me.

Myself Departing

My hair went away in the night while I was sleeping.
It sauntered along the avenue asking, "Why
should I commit myself to him? I have a personality
of my own." Then my good stiff prick went, too.
It opened the window and climbed down the escape,
complaining, "I want to be with someone younger."
The floor was no longer a place for urgent love.
The pretty body I wanted no longer galloped over me,
shouting, "Open, open!" Then fire erupted over
a vast inward terrain that wasn't happiness.
People are always abandoning something; they feel
they haven't been allowed to grow. Though my eyes
leaked, my fingers, cracked from thirst, dried them.
The ring was gone, but the finger lived.

V

FROM

BLIZZARD

Face of the Bee

Staggering out of a black-red peony,
where you have been hiding all morning
from the frigid air, you regard me smearing
jam on dark toast. Suddenly, I am waving
my arms to make you go away. No one
is truly the owner of his own instincts,
but controlling them—this is civilization.
I thank my mother and father for this.
After they died, there were replacements
whose force upon my life I cannot measure.
With your fuzzy black face, do you see me—
a cisgender male—metabolizing
life into language, like nectar sipped
up and regurgitated into gold?

On Peeling Potatoes

When I peel potatoes, I put my head down,
as if I am still following orders and being loyal
to my commander. I feel a connection across
time to others putting their heads down
in fatigued thought, as if this most natural
act signified living the way I wanted to,
with the bad spots cut out, and eluding
my maker. Instead of cobwebs, tumult,
and dragons, I experience an abundance
of good things, like sunlight leaking through
tall pines in the backyard. I say to myself:
This is certainly not a grunt's knowledge—
perception of a potato as my own soul—
but a sturdy, middle-aged, free man's.

Black Mushrooms

For Seamus Heaney

The entire fungus world is wild and unnatural.
In cottony growths on the forest floor, a few spores alight,
and, if moisture and food are available, swell and grow
into protuberances, with elongating stems and raised
caps, gills, and veils. It is not always possible to identify them—
white, black, or tan; torn, bruised, or crushed—
some with squat fruit-bodies, others lacelike. Even the luxury-
    loving
Romans savored their palatal starlight. Sometimes,
when I'm suffocating from an atmosphere of restraint
within myself, I fry them up in butter, with pepper and salt,
and forget where the hurt came from. Instead, I experience
desire creating desire, and then some milder version
of a love that is temporary and guiltless, as if twigs
and bark were giving my life back its own flavor.

Lingonberry Jam

What a wondrous thing to suddenly be alive
eating Natalie's lingonberry jam from Alaska,
where she picked the fruit herself with one seeing eye.
In this tumultuous world we're living in—
with the one-hour news loop—my thoughts
linger, more and more, on the darkish side
as I sit at the table with Mr. & Mrs. Spork,
who still ask me, *Are you married yet?*
But Natalie's lingonberry jam pierces right
through into some deep, essential place,
where I am my own master and no sodomy
laws exist, and where, like a snowflake,
or a bee lost amid the posies, I feel
autonomous, blissed-out, and real.

To a Snail

Like flesh, or consciousness inhabited
by flesh, willful, bold, *très chic*, the skin
on your gelid body is brownish from age
and secretes viscid slime from your flat
muscular foot, like script, as if Agnes Martin
had wed Caravaggio, and then, after rainfall,
you ran away, crossing a wet road with Fiats
rushing past. Where is your partner?
Contemplating your tentacles and house,
gliding on a trace of mucus from some
dark stone to who knows where,
why do I feel happiness? It's a long game—
the whole undignified, insane attempt at living—
so I've relocated you to the woods.

Jelly

For Betty Bird and Susan Thompson

Rubbing the bristle brush across his backbone,
securing the bridle, riding his stretched-out body
on the dirt road to town (past the Texaco station),
and following his head through hair grass and cornflowers,
she was some kind of in-between creature,
browned from the sun. To the sightless,
at the State School for the Deaf and Blind,
knowledge came in small words—under, over,
next to, inside—but it was the clip-clop of Jelly's
hooves, his fragrant mane and muscle memory
that carried her forward, hollering, "Run, Jelly. Run!"
Then, with one soft-firm "Whoa," he did, though she
was only six, her child-hands gripping the reins tight,
hearts thumping a testimony to the love feeling.

To the Oversoul

Halfway down the grassy path,
a cemetery cat, a horse chestnut,
a marble angel. "This is my friend,"
I wrote on blue-lined paper. "Please take
care of her. The tumor-board didn't help her.
Why did they treat her like that? She has
no mother or father. What others call off-
spring, these were her talismanic poems.
It doesn't take a lot of strength to hang on.
It takes strength to let go. Please tell that
to the Oversoul." Then the mommy
cat humped my leg, meowing: *Bliss,*
loss, trembling, compulsion, desire,
& disease are covered with grass now.

The Party Tent

The tent men arrived bearing sledgehammers
and were young enough to be my sons.
After rolling out the canvas, they drove rods
into the earth, heaving and grunting, with blow after blow.
When they raised the center pole, the tent went up,
with tightening ropes, and I felt my heart accelerate,
my heart that is nothing but a specialized nerve,
which my mind feeds off.
                                        Someday, nature's undertakers—
beetles, maggots, and bottle flies—will carry it
toward the sun. Tomorrow, after the tent is gone,
a crew will remove the damaged sod,
aerate what's underneath, and apply a topdressing
of new sandy soil. Like musical notes or forms
of rock, everything will be forgotten.

At the Grave of Robert Lowell

On this tenth day of the year, I play Stravinsky
and sip vodka from a paper cup, taking in the view.
Tendrils twining, leaves rippling, guts absorbing nutrients,
brains marked by experience—all of it is dust now.
He, she, all of them lie under sod, men and women
no longer rivals in love. Bodies grow old and fester.
History is like an Impressionist painting, a variegated
landscape of emotional colors. As night falls,
owls, bats, and hedgehogs come out to hunt.
I take joy in considering my generation. I rewrite
to be read, though I feel shame acknowledging it.
Scattered among imposing trees, the ancient
and the modern intersect, spreading germs of pain
and happiness. I curl up in my fleece and drink.

Recycling

When the environment deteriorates,
we do, too, so I compost coffee grounds
and recycle green glass. The cadaver goes
to a friend's maggot farm where it is turned
into chicken feed. Where there is danger,
there also grows something to save us.
Bathers at the lake act upon their urges
and create an atmosphere of freedom. The thieving
financier becomes a priest with a shelter.
Me—I have no biological function and grow
like a cabbage without making divisions
of myself. Still, I have such a precise feeling
of the weeks recycling, of a stranger's arrival,
and the tumult righting itself.

Paris Is My Seroquel

Long may I savor your organ meats
and stinky cheeses, endure your pompous
manners, breathe your gentle gardens,
wake up—beyond boredom and daydream—
under your gray skies, smiling politely
at so many dull faces passing me by,
I, who am normally so restrictive,
except in relation to him I once loved
(worn and dangerous now), each day,
kneeling down as some strange energy
penetrates my forehead, I, striving to draw
nearer to you, and to your stones, without nervousness
or regret, as all the beauty of the world
seems to touch my haunches and hooves.

Doves

Gray and white, as if with age, or some preserving
of the past, as in Beowulf, our hoary ancestor,
hoary as in a bat or a willow, or the venerable
hoary dove that flew straight into my picture
window today and then lay dead on the front porch.
We buried it—in some distorted version of its normal self—
folded in a white cloth napkin in the backyard.
Still soft enough to be cut into like a cabbage, I thought,
I'm glad I'm not dead. Listen to them now,
higher up in the trees, biting and scratching,
with their unmistakable twitch of life. *Don't fear
nothing*, their twittering voices cry. The true spirit
of living isn't eating greedily, or reflection, or
even love, but dissidence, like an ax of stone.

Goya

Three corpses bound to a tree stump,
castrated, one without arms, its head impaled
on a branch. A dark impression, richly inked,
with a delicate burnishing of figures. Pondering it,
I feel like a worm worming. If I want the truth,
I must seek it out. The line between the inner
and outer erodes, and I become a hunter putting
my face down somewhere on a path between
two ways of being—one kindly and soft;
the other an executioner. Later, out in the plaza,
I light a cigarette and have a long pull,
with small exhales, taking the measure
of my own hand, its lustrous hairy
knuckles dinged from grinding meat.

Weeping Cherry

On a plateau, with little volcanic mountains,
a muddy river, dangerous when the snow melts,
a fertile valley, cattle breeders, and a music academy,
a tall, handsome, agile people, with straight black hair
and an enterprising spirit, lived peaceably. Though
there had never been hatred between the races,
after a quarrel over local matters, massacres came.
Men, women, and children robbed and deported—
an evacuation, they called it. Heads impaled on branches.
Mounds of corpses, like grim flowers knotted together.
A passing ship transported a few to a distant port,
where Mother was born, though now she, too,
has vanished into the universe, and the cold browns
the weeping cherry, vivid red mixed with blue.

Migrants Devouring the
Flesh of a Dead Horse

Since there's no time for grinding or cooking,
it's best not to drag the parts too far.
As the solitary knife goes in and out,
the mama is exhausted but also rather mild
in her expression, and the baby resembles
a seahorse compelled to know something painful.
No one appears left out—stabbing, licking, or chewing—
or sees the texture of the animal's insides
mirrored in the fluttering of cloth, not lightness
or delicacy, but something more basic,
related to the moist earth. Once this horse ornamented
a field, with its flexible limbs and nuzzling head.
Eat me, it neighs now. The tree of life
is greater than all the helicopters of death.

Super Bloom

America, like a monstrous sow
vomiting cars and appliances into a green ooze
of dollar bills, where is my America?
Agnostic and uninsured, I eat celery, onions,
and garlic—my Holy Trinity of survival. I go
to the desert and celebrate death-life, picking a nosegay
for my room at the Motel 6. You said you would always
tell the truth, Mr. President, but that was a lie, so I'm
pressing my white face to your White House door,
a kind of pig keeper with an urge for happiness.
At the Morbidity Conference, they said we can't know
our own strength. They said we're like roses sprayed
with pesticide. They said one man in a long black car
can't ever really empty out the fullness.

Haiku

After the sewage flowed into the sea
and took the oxygen away, the fishes fled,
but the jellies didn't mind. They stayed
and ate up the food the fishes left behind.
I sat on the beach in my red pajamas
and listened to the sparkling foam,
like feelings being fustigated. Nearby,
a crayfish tugged on a string. In the distance,
a man waved. Unnatural cycles seemed to be
establishing themselves, without regard to our lives.
Deep inside, I could feel a needle skip:

Autumn dark.
Murmur of the saw.
Poor humans.

Pheasant

After espresso, friendly banter, and cold
meats; after the shots taken, the near misses,
and more shots; after frenzy in thick woods,
barking pointers, and sprays of grapeshot;
after the trembling, hollering, and retrieving;
after a long table of antipasti, slow-cooked beans,
and tarts served alongside fruit—the pheasant
lay gutted or hung up for moist roasting.
Preferring to run rather than fly, timid around men,
how they startled upward with a wing-whir.
Now I eat what is caught with my own hands
like my father, and feel confused. The charm
flees. I want my life to be borrowing and
paying back. I don't want to be a gun.

On Pride

(after Apollinaire)

I lived in a rooming house then
and tried to be good but was a real
disappointment. A man without cunning
is like an empty matchbox. I can't remember
now the sad, slow procession of words
between us. Only the hurt. Plug the hole
if the patient is bleeding, I thought.
If you do the right thing in the first three minutes
you'll survive. So we put ice cubes on our napes.
My pride was like a giant, oblong
pumpkin. My words were farting on stone.
Then I kissed you until your face became red.
I can't remember now where the words flew off to,
but what an awful hurt.

Keep Me

I found a necktie on the street, a handmade
silk tie from an Italian designer. *Keep me*,
it pleaded from the trash. There's probably
a story it could tell me of calamity days long ago.
Then yesterday, tying a Windsor knot around
my neck, I heard voices, "Why have you got
that old tie on?" Suddenly, Mason, Roy, Jimmy,
and Miguel were pulling at my arms, like it was
the '80s again, a darksome decade, with another
hard-right president. My lips were not yet content
with stillness. We were on our way home
from a nightclub. "I adore you," Miguel moaned,
"but have to return now. Remember
death ends a life, not a relationship."

Epivir, d4T, Crixivan

The new disease came, but not without warning.
The drugs were a toxic combo that kept the sick going
another year. I loved how you talked in your sleep
about free will. Your clothes smelled, but the blood
levels were normal. Now I have seen the sun god:
this is what I thought when I first saw you—the face,
the bearing—but perfection of form meant nothing
to you, and we were all just souls carrying around
a corpse. I smoked cannabis while the government slept.
Drug companies held parties in Arizona and Florida.
The profit motive always thrives. To those who didn't
sell well in the bars, it felt like *Revenge of the Nerds*.
Goaded by your hand, I wrote poems, an essence
squeezed out of this matter, memory now.

Ginger and Sorrow

My skin is the cover of my body.
It keeps me bound to my surroundings.
It is the leather over my spine.
It is the silk over the corneas of my eyes.
Where I am hairless, at the lips and groin,
there is pinkness and vulnerability.
Despite a protective covering of horny skin,
there is no such problem with my fingers,
whose ridges and grooves are so gratifying
to both the lover and the criminologist.
I think perhaps the entire history
of me is here—viper of memory,
stab of regret, red light of oblivion.
Hell would be living without them.

Rice Pudding

Hansel and Gretel were picking strawberries
and listening to a bronze cuckoo.
As the forest mist thickened,
Hansel snuggled up to his little sister,
admitting they were lost.
                         They were the children
of a broom maker who drank too much.
They did not understand that a wife
is to a husband what the husband makes her,
or that even in our misery life goes on.
Squirrels play. Bees forage. Hemlocks bow.

Sitting at the kitchen table, I eat yesterday's meat,
peas and carrots, with a bowl of rice pudding.
Now that you are dead, my stubborn heart lives.

Blizzard

As soon as I am doing nothing,
I am not able to do anything,
existing quietly behind lock and key,
like a cobweb's mesh.

It's 4 a.m.

The voices of birds do not multiply into a force.
The sun does not engross from the East.
A fly roams the fingers on my right hand
like worms. Somewhere, in an empty room, a phone rings.
On the street, a bare tree shadows a brownstone.
(Be precise about objects, but reticent about feelings,
the master urged.)

I need everything within
to be livelier. Infatuation, sadism, lust: I remember them,

but memory of feeling is not feeling,
a parasite is not the meat it lived on.

Dandelions (III)

Everyone has secrets—moments that change them.
I tell my secrets to some dandelions hugging the lichen-like turf.
He was doing lines on a mirror and had sugar spots on his nose.
It made him seem focused, with a conversational prowess.
I was in some kind of low-oxygen dead zone. You flee or suffocate.
Only jellies survive. Maybe I was afraid of emptiness—*horror*
    vacui.
After the insufflation of the only real love of his life, he texted a
    stranger.
I was brooding. You will never disembarrass yourself from this.
Then my love-hate carried me home. There, I'm done with it,
I thought, full of my own idea, like transparent glass
made less invisible by a light that goes straight through it
and then bends into a spectrum. Or like a winter day,
when a low bluish sunlight memorializes everything
and long shadows darken out to a void.

On Friendship

Lately, remembering anything involves an ability
to forget something else. Watching the news,
I writhe and moan; my mind is not itself.
Lying next to a begonia from which black ants come and go,
I drink a vodka. Night falls. This seems a balm
for wounds that are not visible in the gaudy daylight.
Sometimes, a friend cooks dinner; our lives commingle.
In loneliness, I fear me, but in society I'm like a soldier
kneeling on soft mats. Everything seems possible,
as when I hear birds that awaken at 4 a.m. or see
a veil upon a face. Beware the heart is lean red meat.
The mind feeds on this. I carry on my shoulder
a bow and arrow for protection. I believe whatever
I do next will surpass what I have done.

Corpse Pose

Waiting for a deceased friend's cat to die
is almost unbearable. "This is where you live now,"
I explain. "Please stop crying." But he is like a widower
in some kind of holding pattern around a difficult truth.
His head, his bearing, his movements are handsome to me,
a kind of permanent elsewhere devoted to separation and death.
"Please, let's try to forget, dear. We need each other."
I feel I want to tell him something, but I'm not sure what.
So much about life doesn't make sense. Each night,
I do the corpse pose, and he ponders me, with his corpse face,
licking his coat. The Egyptians first tamed his kind.
Their dead were buried in galleries closed up with stone slabs.
When my friend and I were young,
we tramped through woods of black oaks.

Man and Kitten

It is such a curiously pleasant thing to hold
the tenseness of a kitten—barefooted
and subordinate—with soft, assertive tongue.
Teaching it what I know, I think, It loves me.
A man is very nearly a god, a kitten nothing.
A man is self-praising, answering to nobody.
A kitten chooses slavery over hunger.
Tonight: mushrooms and bean curd,
with lemon sauce. A kitten will eat anything.
Its life is mine now. It seems to like this.
It doesn't know my phone doesn't ring.
It doesn't know it reveals my life in a new light,
even secured by a string. Suddenly, there is
trance, illumination, spectacle.

Kayaking on the Charles

I don't really like the ferries that make the water a scary vortex,
or the blurry white sun that blinds me, or the adorable small
    families
of distressed ducklings that swim in a panic when a speedboat cuts
through, spewing a miasma into the river, but I love the Longfellow
Bridge's towers that resemble the silver salt and pepper canisters
on my kitchen table. They belonged to Mother. The Department
of Transportation is restoring the bridge masonry now. Paddling
    under
its big arches, I feel weary, as memory floats up, ignited by cigarette
butts thrown down by steelworkers. I want to paddle away, too.
Flies investigate my bare calves, and when I slap them hard
I realize they are so happy. I'm their amusement. Sometimes
memories involve someone I loved. A rope chafes a cleat.
I want my life to be post–pas de deux now. Lord, look at me,
hatless, with naked torso, sixtyish, paddling alone upriver.

NEW

POEMS

Mouse in the Grocery

There are no bacon strips this morning
so a mouse ponders a pound of sugar.
A mouse wants what a mouse wants,
salt-cured pork instead of soluble carbs.
A mouse is like a heart: it sleeps in winter;
it knows uncertain love; it appears to have no gender.
Now this mouse regards a woman sprinkling water
on lettuce as a man pushes a broom up the aisle.
None of us knows what to expect out there.
Surely pain is to be part of it
and the unwelcome intrusion of the past,
like violent weather that makes a grim chiaroscuro
of the air before a curtain of rainwater falls.
I clutch my basket and push on.

ELF-STORAGE

(White letters on a Bronx warehouse)

The paradoxes and mysteries of elf identity
are not so frightening in storage. Of course,
there are arguments—affectionate and intense—
among the elves, each one grappling with basic
questions of love and elfhood. What can *I* mean
to another elf? Which elf do I want to be with?
What kind of elf do I want to be? The pleasures
of opening up emotionally as one elf to another
do not really exist in storage. Many elves with
a deep and long-standing investment in elfhood
deteriorate. A warehouse is not a good place
for an elf of prominence. It is more a place
for the brave little elves who can accept
a vague and shapeless existence.

Time and Weather

Now the spell is broken. A gold light traces
a line across the sky, which had been so dark,
without a cloud to be seen from one horizon
to the other. Now darker emotions dissolve.
Violence seems dumb. Things that were come back.
A red bird circles around a bush. A woman
ties the sandal of a child. A new president
speaks of our souls instead of power. Likewise,
the grass upon the mountain trembles
greener, reproducing itself while strug-
gling against human rivals. A friend asks,
"When do we leave for happiness?" Friends
are better than guns. This morning, I eat
cornbread with butter and jam. I walk.

Guns

Stick in the mud, old fart, what are you doing
to get the guns off the street? I am not here to pick
on anyone. But now that they have shot Yosi,
who ground my meat in Hingham, and his shiny pink
meat-truck is for sale, I feel desolate. A gun is
a vengeful machine exacting a price. A gun rejects
stillness. It wants to get off. A man can be vain—
almost like a god—but inside him is a carp biting
the muck of a lake. A man who speaks too softly
gets hit with a big stick and lopes along behind.
A gun is minatory. Still, a week of kindness is greater.
Run, hide, evacuate; don't fire, duck, take cover.
At Yosi's ceremony, his family put a gold cloth on his face.
Self-reliant, autonomous, tough, he lay in a shroud of silk.

Daffodils

Sometimes I arrive with my buds closed,
and I am mistaken for scallions,
but if you cut a half inch from my stems
and put me in water, I open up and release
yellow dust from my petal cups,
like talcum sprinkled on her shoulders
after she bathes and swallows her
third tranquilizer to erase herself,
the sedative piercing right through her
like a small bunch of flowers grasped
by a hand that connects the melancholy
to something in nature urging *Trust me*,
as the blackbirds at dawn trust
the aurora that conquers night.

Glass of Absinthe and Cigarette

This is a poem about a man who is dead.
Sodomy laws treated him like a second-class citizen.
There were ripple effects. With the aid of stimulants,
he spoke like a truthteller and hungered for touch.
Even when repugnant, his disinhibition seemed godlike,
and what came out of him ravished me.
Alas, tolerance builds rapidly, and many lines must be
insufflated to produce that all-is-right-in-the-world euphoria:
"Feeling good. R U there. Come right now."
To keep myself sane,
I fled, dear reader,
but I'd give my kingdom
to see myself in those
dilated black eyes again.

Vetiver

The splash of rain against my windows, as wind lifts it from the
    park,
daffodils gleaming under streetlamps, morning light so full of
    softness and sounds—
a wet cardinal, a distant ambulance—the blue hydrangea on the
    kitchen table,
everything posthumous-seeming, as I read the newspaper in my
    bathrobe,
without a fever, sweat, ache, nausea, exhaustion, cough, or struggle
    to breathe.
Later, stretched out on the bedroom floor, I observe a vivid sky,
    with fluffy clouds,
like the uncut hairs around my ears that give me a less austere,
    Roman look.

Do not think of the abyss, I say to myself.
Soon the lilacs will begin their heavy exhalations in green light,
the lawn will roll out its plush carpet,
and the late-night sky will seem deeper, as the swallows fly
    diagonally into it.

Once again, we'll eat endives and ham, eggs every style, peaches
 in red wine,
and we'll forget our confinement, as the upright robins,
six feet apart, *tuk-tuk-tuk* on the wire.

Sow with Piglets

Here, in a plywood shed, she keeps herself sane
licking her black piglets and kissing their eyes.
She seems so confident, with thoughts running fast.
She makes my day a little better. Each night,
during the well-pig check, her teat-milk carries them
off into themselves, into the single being we adults
know as the source of our own sadness.
But here, under a dispassionate night sky,
in pig-time, with blue moonlight filtering
through the cedars, I ask, Why do you leave
for happiness? Why not stay around awhile?
With muddy sneakers and thick torso,
I feel saner in this place. I've paid my price
and am here for the duration.

Afterword

Twenty years ago, when I was living in the foothills north of Kyoto in two tatami-mat rooms, without possessions except a futon and a wok, I chose to write free verse sonnets in plain speech and to bring to them some of the characteristics of Japanese poetry: the Buddhist notion of dealing less with conceptualized thought than with states of mind and feeling, a sense of social responsibility, a valuing of sincerity over artifice, the use of images as emblems for inner states, and a preoccupation with themes of love. I was studying tea ceremony, and my teachers, wearing kimonos in the old style, made me see that emotions like pride and vanity had no place there, where physical sensations—the feel of tatami, the odor of summer, the sound of water boiling in the kettle, the taste of sugar—were a source of pleasure. I wanted to write poems that conveyed the intensity of my life there—the wildness and innocence, and the freedom. The sonnet—with its infrastructure of highs and lows, with its volta and the idea of transformation, with its asymmetry of lines like the foliage of a tree growing above a trunk, and with its mix of passion and thought—seemed to me about perfect. I believe a poem is a sonnet if it behaves like one, and this doesn't mean rhyming iambic pentameter lines. More important is the psychological dimension, the little fractures and leaps and resolutions the poem enacts.

In a sonnet, the same moves are never performed in exactly the same way. I don't think there is anything sacred or inevitable about the fourteen-line poem called a sonnet. But I do think there is a structural mimesis in the sonnet that replicates thought and emotion, and I am drawn to this. I like watching words and stanzas become characters in a poem along with the psychological drama. I know it's an entirely personal thing, but for some reason the lean, muscular body of the sonnet frees me to be simultaneously dignified and bold, to appear somewhat socialized though what I have to say may be eccentric or unethical, and, most important of all, to have aesthetic power while writing about the tragic situation of the individual in the world.

Acknowledgments

For their encouragement, I am indebted to the editors of the following publications, where poems, sometimes in different form, were originally published.

Alaska Quarterly Review: "Sunflower"

The American Poetry Review: "Goya," "The Lost Bee," and "Mirror"

The American Scholar: "Dandelions (III)," "Face of the Bee," "Keep Me," "On Peeling Potatoes," "Passion," "Seaweed," and "Taxidermied Fawn"

The Atlantic: "Birthday," "Black Camellia," "Dead Wren," "Hens," "Landscape with Deer and Figure," "Pig," and "Quai aux Fleurs"

The Believer: "Legend" and "Super Bloom"

Liberties: "Glass of Absinthe and Cigarette" and "Guns"

Literary Imagination: "Cleaning the Elephant," "Melon and Insects," "Mosquito Mother," "Swans," and "Veil"

Los Angeles Review of Books: "Jelly"

The Nation: "Epivir, d4T, Crixivan" and "Weeping Cherry"

The New Criterion: "To a Snail"

New England Review: "Insomnia" and "Necessary and Impossible"

The New Republic: "Carwash," "ELF-STORAGE," "Embers," "Icarus Breathing," "Mask," and "Orange Hole"

The New York Review of Books: "Black Mushrooms," "Blizzard," "Laughing Monster," "Mechanical Soft," "Mouse in the Grocery," "One Animal," and "Sleeping Soldiers"

The New Yorker: "American Kestrel," "Bowl of Lilacs," "Casablanca Lily," *from* "Chiffon Morning," "Daffodils," "Doves," "Gravity and Center," "Gulls," "Homosexuality," "Kyushu Hydrangea," "Myself with Cats," "On Friendship," "Pillowcase with Praying Mantis," "Poppies," "Radiant Ivory," "Self-Portrait with Red Eyes," "Shrike," "The Tree Cutters," and "White Spine"

The Paris Review: "At the Grave of Robert Lowell," "Corpse Pose," "Haircut," "Kayaking on the Charles," "On Pride," "The Party Tent," "Rice Pudding" (originally published as "No Homecoming"), and "Sycamores" (published here as an untitled prefatory poem)

Ploughshares: "To Sleep"

Poetry: "Haiku"

Poetry Northwest: "Ambulance"

Radcliffe Magazine: "Vetiver"

Salmagundi: "Beach Walk," "Ginger and Sorrow," "Lingonberry Jam," "Man and Kitten," "Migrants Devouring the Flesh of a Dead Horse," "Toxicology," and "Ulro"

Slate: "Crows in Evening Glow," "Dead Mother," "Eating the Peach," and "Original Face"

The Threepenny Review: "Bats," "Broom," "City Horse," "The Flagellation," "Oil & Steel," "Recycling," and "Sow with Piglets"

West 10th: "Hairy Spider"

The Yale Review: "Fish and Watergrass," "The Hare," and "Shaving"

The Best American Poetry 2014 (edited by Terrance Hayes): "City
    Horse"

Disaster Diary (with Susan Unterberg and Jeanne Silverthorne):
    "Time and Weather"

Feathers from the Angel's Wing (edited with an introduction by Dana
    Prescott): "Adam Dying" and "The Flagellation"

*I Know Now in Wonder: 25 Poems from the First 25 Years of the
    Civitella Ranieri Foundation*: "Pheasant"

Love Speaks Its Name: Gay and Lesbian Love Poems (edited by J. D.
    McClatchy), Everyman's Library Pocket Poets: "Peonies"

Motherhood: Poems about Mothers (edited by Carmela Ciuraru),
    Everyman's Library Pocket Poets: *from* "Chiffon Morning"

My Favorite Plant: Writers and Gardeners on the Plants They Love
    (edited by Jamaica Kincaid): "Peonies"

*The Penguin Book of the Sonnet: 500 Years of a Classic Tradition in
    English* (edited by Phillis Levin): *from* "Chiffon Morning"

Poems of Healing (edited by Karl Kirchwey), Everyman's Library
    Pocket Poets: "Morning Glory"

Poems of Paris (edited by Emily Fragos), Everyman's Library Pocket
    Poets: "Paris Is My Seroquel"

Poems of Rome (edited by Karl Kirchwey), Everyman's Library
    Pocket Poets: "Arte Povera"

Poems Poets Poetry (edited by Helen Vendler), 2nd ed.: "Kayaks"

Poems Poets Poetry (edited by Helen Vendler), 3rd ed.: "Carwash"

Index of Titles and First Lines

Titles are in *italics*.
First lines are in plain text.